W9-BXV-197

Auston Matthews

By Julia Sillett

CRABTREE
PUBLISHING COMPANY
WWW.CRABTREEBOOKS.COM

CRABTREE
PUBLISHING COMPANY
WWW.CRABTREEBOOKS.COM

Author: Julia Sillett

Editor: Kathy Middleton

Photo research Crystal Sikkens, Ken Wright

Proofreader: Lorna Notsch

Design, and prepress: Ken Wright

Print coordinator: Katherine Berti

Photo Credits

Alamy: title page, ©Cal Sport Media; p 5, ©WENN Ltd;

Getty: pp 4, 13, ©Minas Panagiotakis / Stringer; p 7, ©Bill Wippert; pp 8, 27 ©Bruce Bennett; p 10, ©P Angers; p 15, ©RONI REKOMAA; p 16, ©Bill Wippert; p 17, ©Jeff Vinnick; p 18, ©Andre Ringuette; p 20, ©Eliot J. Schechter; pp 22, 23, ©Norm Hall; p 24, ©Steve Russell; pp 25, 26, ©Kevin Sousa

Icon Sportswire: Cover, Julian Avram; p 12, ©Tim Vizer

Keystone: p 9, © JE1; p 14, © Melanie Duchene; p 28, © Nicholas T. Loverde

Next Generation Hockey: p 11 BorisDorozhenko

Shutterstock: p 19, Featureflash Photo Agency

Every effort has been made to trace copyright holders and to obtain their permission for use of copyright material. The authors and publishers would be pleased to rectify any error or omission in future editions. All the Internet addresses given in this book were correct at the time of going to press. The author and publishers regret any inconvenience caused if addresses have changed or sites have ceased to exist, but can accept no responsibility for any such changes.

Library and Archives Canada Cataloguing in Publication

Sillett, Julia, author
        Auston Matthews / Julia Sillett.

(Superstars!)
Includes index.
Issued in print and electronic formats.
ISBN 978-0-7787-4829-8 (hardcover).--
ISBN 978-0-7787-4844-1 (softcover).--
ISBN 978-1-4271-2092-2 (HTML)

        1. Matthews, Auston, 1997- --Juvenile literature.
2. Hockey players--United States--Biography--Juvenile literature.
I. Title. II. Series: Superstars! (St. Catharines, Ont.)

GV848.5.M375S55 2018   j796.962092   C2018-900270-0
                                                          C2018-900271-9

Library of Congress Cataloging-in-Publication Data

CIP available at the Library of Congress

Crabtree Publishing Company
www.crabtreebooks.com   1-800-387-7650

Printed in the U.S.A./052018/BG20180327

Copyright © **2018 CRABTREE PUBLISHING COMPANY.** All rights reserved. No part of this publication may be reproduced, stored in a retrieval system or be transmitted in any form or by any means, electronic, mechanical, photocopying, recording, or otherwise, without the prior written permission of Crabtree Publishing Company. In Canada: We acknowledge the financial supportof the Government of Canada through the Canada Book Fund for our publishing activities.

Published in Canada
Crabtree Publishing
616 Welland Ave.
St. Catharines, ON
L2M 5V6

Published in the United States
Crabtree Publishing
PMB 59051
350 Fifth Avenue, 59th Floor
New York, New York 10118

Published in the United Kingdom
Crabtree Publishing
Maritime House
Basin Road North, Hove
BN41 1WR

Published in Australia
Crabtree Publishing
3 Charles Street
Coburg North
VIC 3058

CONTENTS

Words that are defined in the glossary are in
bold type the first time they appear in the text.

He Shoots. He Scores!

It's October 14, 2017, and the Toronto Maple Leafs are playing the Montreal Canadiens in their fifth game of the season. Auston Matthews is beginning his second season playing center for the Maple Leafs, who have lost the last 14 games they've played against the Canadiens. Needless to say, the pressure is on. It's the middle of the first period, and the score is tied at 1−1.

Leafs center Nazem Kadri takes a blow to the wrist and skates off the ice in pain. Auston Matthews jumps from the bench to replace Kadri. Auston immediately takes control of the puck, moving it from one end of the rink to the other, all on his own. With quick thinking and precision, he whips the puck. It passes the defense, then the goaltender. It's a goal!

Auston scored two goals against the Montreal Canadiens, helping the Maple Leafs win the game 4 to 3.

A Shot at Greatness

Since his very first game in the National Hockey League (NHL), number 34, Auston Matthews, has brought something special to the ice. His name might be new to the NHL world, but through his work ethic and natural talent, Auston quickly gained the respect of many devoted hockey fans. He was **drafted** into the NHL in 2016 as the first overall pick of **rookie** players, and has been impressing fans, teammates, coaches, and competitors ever since.

Auston's hockey skills are as unique as his journey to the NHL. His inspiring story has made many people wonder how this young man from the desert state of Arizona became a superstar on the ice. However, despite the odds, he has grown up to join the ranks of his childhood hockey idols, Shane Doan and Daniel Brière.

When Auston Matthews was drafted in 2016, he was the first American to be selected first in the NHL Drafts since Patrick Kane in 2007.

A Hockey Hero Is Born

Auston Matthews was born in San Ramon, California, on September 17, 1997. His father, Brian, is from California, and his mother, Ema, is originally from Mexico. Auston is the middle child in the family. He has an older sister, Alexandria, and a younger sister, Breyana. When Auston was only a few months old, his family moved to Scottsdale, Arizona, where Auston spent the remainder of his childhood.

A love of sports runs in Auston's family. His great-uncle Wes Matthews played in the AFL (American Football League). Auston got his first taste of hockey when his father and Uncle Billy took him to watch the Phoenix Coyotes play. He was two years old. Unfortunately, his Uncle Billy passed away when Auston was young, but his uncle's love of hockey clearly made a huge impression on him.

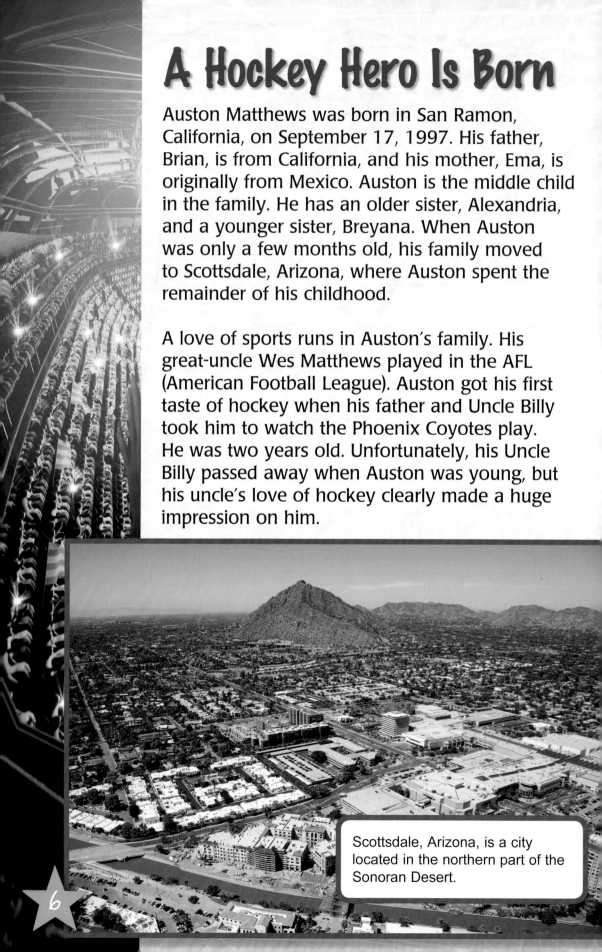

Scottsdale, Arizona, is a city located in the northern part of the Sonoran Desert.

Home Runs or Slap Shots?

Auston's father had a passion for baseball, which he passed on to Auston. By age six, Auston decided he wanted to play hockey, too. His parents didn't know much about the sport, but they could see how much he wanted to play. For a while, Auston played both sports. He enjoyed baseball and was quite good. However, as he got older, baseball practice started overlapping with hockey practice, and he couldn't play both sports. He decided to give up baseball and pursue his hockey career.

Auston is reminded of his childhood as he warms up before throwing the ceremonial pitch at a Buffalo Bisons baseball game in 2016.

" He Said It "

"I think he loved baseball. But there was too much standing around for him. If he could have batted every 15 seconds he would have loved it. Waiting around for the pitcher to throw the ball, it wasn't active enough for him."

—Brian Matthews in *The New York Times*, December 26, 2014.

Hockey Dad

Auston's dedication to hockey made him stand out among the rest. He was always eager for more ice time, so after his own games he would stay at the arena hoping for another team to be short a player. Then, he would volunteer to fill the extra spot on the team. The games were played on a small ice rink and were always 3-on-3. This gave Auston more time with the puck, and he learned how to move it around the other players in a tight space. It never bothered him that some of the players were bigger and older than he was.

Auston's father could see how much his son loved this game. When Auston started focusing all his time on hockey, Brian began learning everything he could about the sport. In his late 30s, Brian even began taking skating lessons, so he could help Auston practice on the ice.

Brian Matthews hugs his son after he's picked first in the 2016 NHL drafts.

They Call Him Papi

Auston's mother knew almost nothing about hockey, but she wanted Auston to follow his dream and did everything she could to make that happen. She even worked two jobs to help cover the costs of the **tournaments**, equipment, and travel expenses.

Ema has always called her son "Papi." It is a Spanish word used in an affectionate way to refer to a son. The nickname caught on. Not only did his family start calling him Papi, but so did all his friends and teammates. Even at age 18, while Auston was training to become a professional hockey player, he was still called Papi by all his teammates.

Auston's mother Ema accompanies him to the 2017 NHL Awards and tells reporters, "I am a very proud mom."

She Said It

"I'm just a mom who is very proud of my family and I get very passionate with everything our kids do and I don't hide my emotions"
—Ema Matthews in an interview with Ryan O'Leary from the International Ice Hockey Federation (IIHF), October 10, 2016

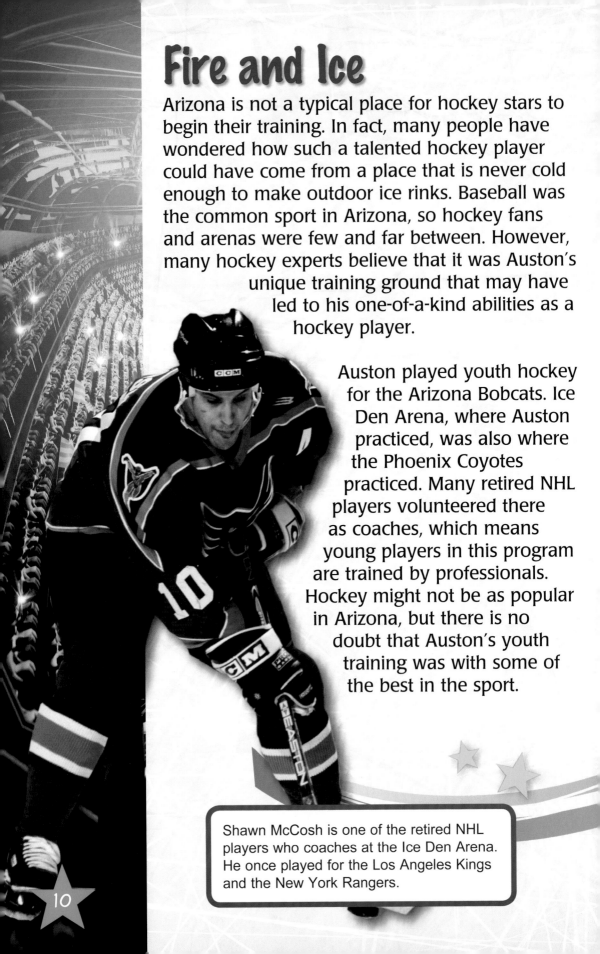

Fire and Ice

Arizona is not a typical place for hockey stars to begin their training. In fact, many people have wondered how such a talented hockey player could have come from a place that is never cold enough to make outdoor ice rinks. Baseball was the common sport in Arizona, so hockey fans and arenas were few and far between. However, many hockey experts believe that it was Auston's unique training ground that may have led to his one-of-a-kind abilities as a hockey player.

Auston played youth hockey for the Arizona Bobcats. Ice Den Arena, where Auston practiced, was also where the Phoenix Coyotes practiced. Many retired NHL players volunteered there as coaches, which means young players in this program are trained by professionals. Hockey might not be as popular in Arizona, but there is no doubt that Auston's youth training was with some of the best in the sport.

Shawn McCosh is one of the retired NHL players who coaches at the Ice Den Arena. He once played for the Los Angeles Kings and the New York Rangers.

Coached by the Best

One of Auston's coaches was Boris Dorozhenko from Ukraine. Many people in Arizona's hockey community thought some of Boris's teaching techniques were unusual. Players aren't allowed to practice with pucks at first. Pucks are given to students as rewards for skill-building. But Auston's family supported Boris's methods and saw how they impacted Auston's skills. Boris became a close friend of the family and even lived with Auston's grandparents. Thanks to Boris, Auston got a chance to play in an important international **Pee-Wee** tournament for a Ukrainian team! They needed a player for their games in Quebec, Canada, and Boris wanted to see Auston show his skills to a new audience. It took a little convincing, but eventually Auston's parents agreed to let him do it. Despite a little homesickness, Auston was a star during this tournament.

Boris Dorozhenko and Auston in training

11

Persistent in the Face of Challenges

While playing with the Arizona Bobcats, Auston had racked up 55 goals and 100 points in 48 games. His obvious talent was starting to be noticed by important people in the hockey world. The summer before he turned 16, coach Don Granato invited him to try out for the US National Team Development Program (USNTDP) in Ann Arbor, Michigan. Only 22 of the top junior players are accepted each year. To no one's surprise, Auston won a spot in the Under-17 Team (U17).

However, Auston was quickly faced with a challenge. In 2013, he broke his **femur** while playing in his second game for the U17 National Team. As discouraging as this was at the time, Auston said afterward that it made him stronger mentally and as a person. After surgery on his femur, he was determined to come back as quickly as he could and stronger than ever.

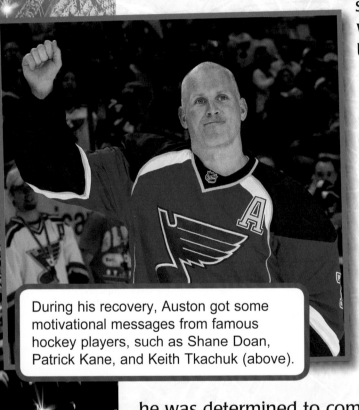

During his recovery, Auston got some motivational messages from famous hockey players, such as Shane Doan, Patrick Kane, and Keith Tkachuk (above).

He Said It

"He came back quicker than anybody I've seen come back from that…it was remarkable."
—Keith Tkachuk, quoted on ESPN.com, December 23, 2015

Not Your Average Teenager

And what a comeback it was! As part of the USNTDP, Auston played for the US Hockey League, U17 National Team, and U18 National Team. Auston went on to help his U18 team bring home gold medals two years in a row—at the Ice Hockey U18 World Championship in Finland in 2014 and Switzerland in 2015. At the 2015 tournament, he was named the tournament's Most Valuable Player (MVP), leading all players in goals and points. In his second year in the program, Auston set the US U18 record for goals and points in one season, surpassing Patrick Kane's record. Auston was a busy teenager, and at age 16, he was being homeschooled, learning at a faster pace so he could enroll in college early and play in the National Collegiate Athletic Association (NCAA) league for college hockey. His high school years may have looked different than those of most teenagers, but his parents and his coaches all commented on the discipline and work ethic he demonstrated during those years. Auston was determined to become better and better every day.

At an exhibition game in Austria in 2015, Auston spotted Sidney Crosby as they were both taping their sticks. The sighting inspired Auston to want to move beyond the juniors as soon as he could.

Big Dreams

At age 18, Auston's story took another interesting turn. Most NHL hockey players will go on from the US National Team Development Program to the WHL or NCAA. Auston could have done either; however, he had other plans. He wanted to play professionally. Auston wasn't old enough to be considered for the 2015 NHL Draft—he missed the cut-off by only two days! Instead, he spent the 2015–2016 season playing for the Zurich Lions in Switzerland's National League A, the country's highest level of hockey. Auston moved to Switzerland, and his mom and sister came with him.

Languages

During his time in Switzerland, Auston picked up a little of the native language, called Suisse-German. This added to his list of languages, which already included English and Spanish.

Auston appreciated having his mother and older sister there after spending so much time away from his family while playing for the USNTDP. Ema was dedicated to her son's nutrition. She made meals that provided him with the energy he needed to keep up with his busy schedule. His sister Alexandria took time off from school to help her younger brother stay on track with his own online studies.

Auston got professional experience playing for the Zurich Lions. This helped him reach his goal of playing in the NHL.

Player Beyond His Years

While playing in Switzerland, Auston gained excellent experience and proved himself worthy to play in the NHL. He got 24 goals in 36 games! On October 9, 2015, Auston scored the game-winning goal in Zurich's game against the team's rival, Davos. The crowd went wild! They cheered his name over and over again, which in Switzerland, means that fans want that player to return to the ice and wave to them. When this happened, Auston was flustered and didn't know how to respond! He eventually realized that they wanted him to come back out, so he went back and shared a moment with the crowd. Auston Matthews was only 18 years old when he arrived in Switzerland, but his coach and his teammates have commented how mature and professional he was during his time playing for Zurich.

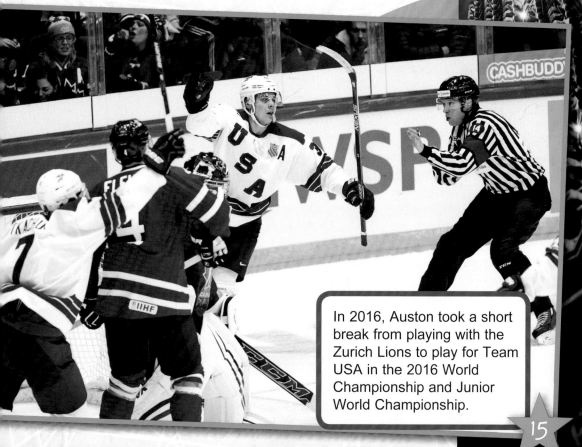

In 2016, Auston took a short break from playing with the Zurich Lions to play for Team USA in the 2016 World Championship and Junior World Championship.

Number One Pick

Auston was now catching the attention of the NHL community. Every year in June, the NHL holds a draft, during which teams take turns selecting young, new players from junior leagues or professional European leagues. Before the 2016 draft began, people were already predicting that 19-year-old Auston Matthews would be the first pick.

The 2016 draft was held in Buffalo, New York. A few lucky prospects, including Auston, had been selected to participate in some activities during the couple days leading up to the draft. They got the chance to practice baseball with the Buffalo Bisons, had a tour of Niagara Falls on the *Maid of the Mist*, and visited Roswell Park Cancer Institute, where they met with some patients.

Before the 2016 draft, Auston took part in the Top Prospects Hockey Clinic, at which he helped young hockey players learn various skills.

Looking for a Hero

The Toronto Maple Leafs won the draft lottery, which meant the team got to be the first to pick a new player. As expected, Auston's name was the first one announced, and the crowd in the stadium went wild! Maple Leaf fans were filled with hope at the thought of having a promising player like Auston on their favorite team. He hugged his parents and sisters before heading on stage to put on the Maple Leafs jersey.

The Maple Leafs have not won a Stanley Cup since 1967, and in the 12 years before Auston joined, the Leafs only made the playoffs twice. The team was in need of a change. They had begun rebuilding the team to include new, young talent who could lead them to victory. Auston Matthews was of this rebuild era, and he had people wondering if he was the hockey hero they had been waiting for.

Team Player

Auston was grateful for all the support he was receiving, but he wanted it to be known that, above all else, he was a team player. His goal going forward was to make the team better.

Not Just Beginner's Luck

It is October 16, 2016, and Auston Matthews positions himself at center ice to take the face-off in his first NHL game. The Leafs are playing the Ottawa Senators. Some may be expecting a typical rookie game from Auston. They have no idea they are about to witness the making of hockey history.

In the NHL, when a player scores three goals in one game, he earns what is called a "hat trick." Fans often throw their hats onto the ice to celebrate a player's hat trick. It's an exciting moment for any hockey player, but for Auston, the crowds were in shock. Cheers rang and hats went flying when he completed a hat trick before the end of the second period. Auston wasn't finished yet either. He made history when he scored again, becoming the first player in hockey's **modern era** to score four goals in his first NHL game.

He Scores

Craig Anderson, goaltender for the Ottawa Senators, had Auston sign his hockey stick after the game. Auston wrote "Thanks 'FOUR' making my first game memorable," referring to the four goals he let in.

Auston's four goals even seemed to shock his parents— they watched from the stands with disbelief and proud tears in their eyes.

A Challenge for a Champion

While Auston's first game was a thrilling start to his NHL career, he would soon face the challenges that came along with playing with the world's most talented hockey players. He might have made scoring look easy in his first few games, but soon after, he fell into a "scoring slump," as many reporters called it. Auston endured a 13-game run without scoring any goals, and was only able to make three assists. This slump was discouraging. However, even though Auston wasn't scoring any goals on the ice, he was still setting goals for himself in training. He wanted to meet the expectations of his coach, his teammates, the fans, and maybe even more, his own high expectations for himself.

When times are tough, Auston stays motivated by remembering a quote from professional boxer Muhammad Ali. Ali once said, "I hated every minute of training, but I said, Don't quit. Suffer now and live the rest of your life as a champion."

Dad's Got Your Back

Auston's family had seen his perseverance over the years and knew he would make his way out of this slump. His father, who had moved to Toronto to help Auston in his career change, was especially supportive. Brian helped Auston focus on the big picture, rather than the negative media attention. Auston never lost hope. He kept working at the other skills his coach wanted him to practice, and finally, Auston started scoring goals again. He was back in the game!

Head coach of the Toronto Maple Leafs, Mike Babcock, knows that for some players their fathers have been an important part of their professional hockey journeys. To celebrate the sacrifices their families have made, he organizes an annual Father Road Trip, during which team members bring their father or brother along on the road to watch several games.

Mike Babcock cares about the **well-being** of his team and encourages them to be team players on and off the ice.

Team Time

Auston is learning how to take some pressure off and have fun with his teammates. Coach Babcock suggested they find a way to have fun and grow as a team. Their activity of choice was video games, so in their downtime, the team will challenge each other to some virtual competition. (Word has it that Auston is not nearly as talented on the screen as he is on the ice!)

Regardless of his gaming skills, Auston is a valued member of the Toronto Maple Leafs team on and off the ice. The other players speak highly of him, and Auston in turn, always credits his teammates for his success. When he shares the praise with his teammates, he shows that his focus is on the team, not himself.

He Said It

"Auston makes me play better. Auston makes us play better."
—Connor Brown, quoted on nhl.com, January 13, 2017

Home for Christmas

As Christmastime rolled around, Auston was becoming the dominant center Coach Babcock wanted him to be. With more confidence and new skills, Auston was ready to face a new challenge. On December 23, 2016, the Maple Leafs were scheduled to play against the Arizona Coyotes, in Auston's hometown. Ever since Auston first watched a hockey game with his Uncle Billy, he had loved the Coyotes. The Phoenix Coyotes had changed their team name to the Arizona Coyotes in 2014. Auston took the opening face-off against his boyhood idol, Shane Doan. Even though this was an exciting game for Auston, it was business as usual when he was on the ice. During that game, he had an assist, and the Maple Leafs went home for Christmas with a 4−1 victory over the Coyotes.

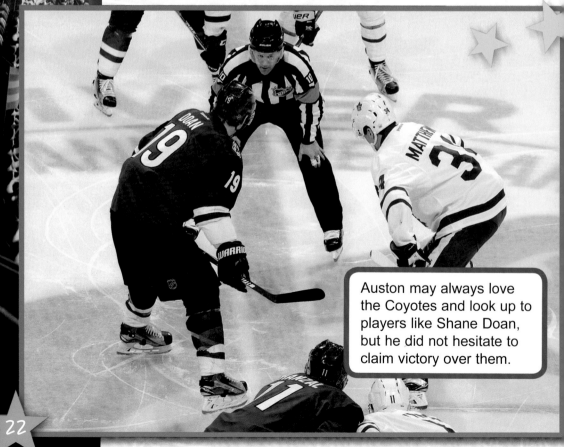

Auston may always love the Coyotes and look up to players like Shane Doan, but he did not hesitate to claim victory over them.

Hometown Hero

Arizona welcomed Auston back with open arms. Some Arizona Coyotes fans even wore Auston Matthews Maple Leafs jerseys to the game out of pride for their hometown hockey star. It was an important game for him, but also for those in his hometown who now look up to him. After the game, he went back out on the ice to meet hundreds of young people who play hockey in Arizona. He told reporters that he wanted to be a role model for young hockey players.

Ron Filion, one of Auston's coaches from his youth, told Auston that they'd had to cancel practices for five different teams that day, because nearly all the players and coaches had purchased tickets to watch Auston play the Coyotes. After that game, Auston drove home with his family to their house in Scottsdale to celebrate Christmas in the warm Arizona weather.

Auston Matthews is an inspiration to youth hockey players in Arizona.

Remembering Uncle Billy

The Toronto Maple Leafs have been making annual visits to cheer up patients at Toronto's SickKids Hospital since the team's earliest seasons in the 1920s. The players use these occasions to visit patients, hand out gifts, and sign photographs for the hospitalized children.

For Auston Matthews, his visits to the SickKids hospital remind him of the man who first ignited his love for hockey—his Uncle Billy. Billy died of **cystic fibrosis** (CF) when Auston was young. The SickKids hospital made an important discovery for CF research in 1989 that improved the quality of life for CF patients. Auston has found a way to recognize this hospital's important work. In addition to joining his team on trips to visit the hospital, Auston has made special visits on his own to spend more time with children who are receiving treatment for cystic fibrosis.

Giving Back

Auston not only spends time with CF patients, he also agreed to act in a video demonstration of a difficult breathing test so children with CF would feel more comfortable with the procedure.

The Leafs team mascot, Carlton the Bear, joins the team on their annual visit to SickKids hospital.

Another Team to Join

On the ice, Auston wears BAUER gear, which is the name of the world's biggest manufacturer of hockey equipment. Shortly before Auston was drafted into the NHL, he agreed to a **sponsorship** deal with BAUER and was listed as one of the company's "Elite Roster of Athletes." This kind of partnership is not only an honor, but the athletes are also paid by the company to wear its gear. In return, the company benefits from superstars wearing its brand in front of millions of people watching the games.

When Auston isn't wearing his number 34 jersey, his fashion choices are inspired by one of his favorite professional athletes, Russell Westbrook. He is an American basketball player in the NBA. Auston often struts into his games wearing a suit and tie, keeping warm with a chunky scarf and tuque.

The BAUER brand can be seen in many places, including Auston's helmet, gloves, and stick.

A Strong Rookie Game

Fans have learned from the Maple Leafs team not to underestimate rookie players. During Auston's first season, his linemates in the 2016–2017 season were a rotation of three other rookie players, including Connor Brown, William Nylander, and Zach Hyman. Rookies are players who have not played in more than 25 NHL games. Leafs coach Mike Babcock has said about the line that although they are young, they are all good players. He later explained why Auston's line works so well together. "[William] right now is playing with those guys, with an elite shot, and really competing at a whole other level. Hyman and Brown work every single day. And Matthews has that skill set we talk about so much."

All-Star

Auston was the only Maple Leaf selected to participate in both the 2017 and 2018 NHL All-Star games. The NHL All-Star game is an exhibition game in which the top players in the league compete against each other.

Auston is seen here celebrating a goal with teammates Zach Hyman and Connor Brown.

Rookie of the Year

Every year, the NHL awards the Calder Memorial Trophy to the Rookie of the Year. The winner is decided by a panel of judges who vote on who they think is the best player in his first NHL year. By the end of the 2016–2017 season, the vote was almost **unanimous**. Auston Matthews won with his impressive record, leading all rookies in goals, points, and shots on goal. Not only was this an outstanding personal accomplishment, it was also a victory for his team. It was the first time in 51 years that a player from the Maple Leafs had won the Calder Trophy. Auston was chosen ahead of the two other talented nominees, Patrik Laine of the Winnipeg Jets and Zach Werenski of the Columbus Blue Jackets. In his speech, Auston humbly congratulated Patrik and Zach on great seasons and thanked everyone who has brought him this far—his family, his coaches, his teammates, and "Leafs Nation," who he calls "the best fans in the league."

Since 1933, the Toronto Maple Leafs have had the most players win the Calder Trophy.

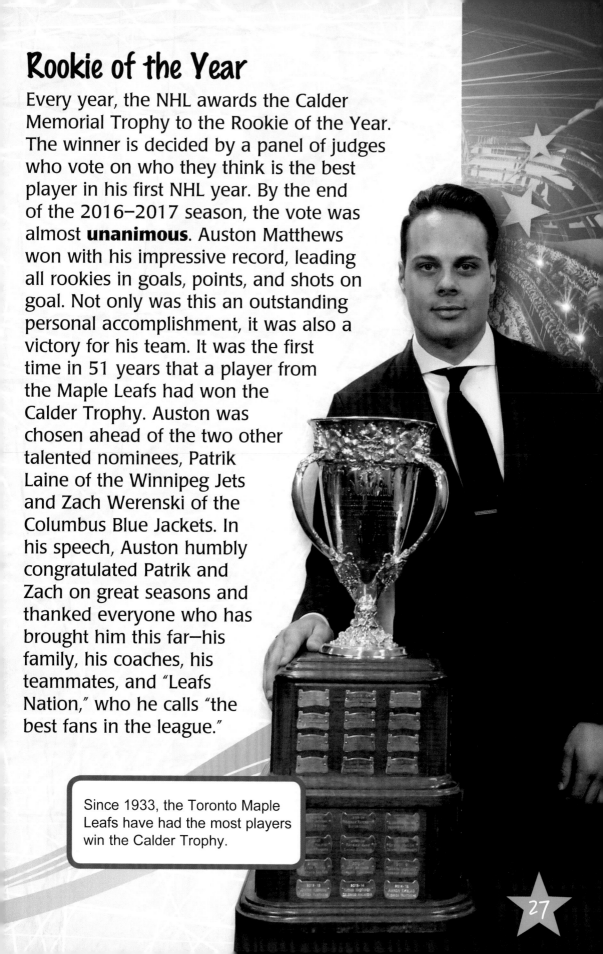

A Franchise Centerman

Coach Babcock has put a lot of faith in Auston's abilities. He was originally going to have Auston play on the **wing**, supporting the center player in his role. However, Auston convinced his coach to let him play center. Auston has said that he wants be a "**franchise** centerman." This title doesn't just mean he wants to be the best player on his team now, but a strong player and a leader for many years to come. A title like this means a lot of hard work, a strong sense of perseverance, and the spirit of a player who cares more for his team than for himself. If anyone is up for the task, it's Toronto Maple Leafs hockey star, Auston Matthews.

He Said It

"I want to be an impact player. I believe I can be a franchise centerman, a No. 1 centerman in the NHL, so that's my ultimate goal"
−Auston Matthews, in *100 Years in Blue and White: A Century of Hockey in Toronto* by Bruce Arthur, June 25, 2016

Timeline

1997: Auston Matthews is born in San Ramon, California, on September 17. His family moves to Arizona when he is a few months old.

2003: 6-year-old Auston starts playing hockey

2011: Auston plays for Arizona Bobcats Under-14 (14U)

2012: Auston plays for Arizona Bobcats Under-16 (16U)

2013: Auston is accepted in USA Hockey's National Team Development Program (USNTDP) in Michigan. He begins as a member of the US National Under-17 Team (U17).

2013: Auston breaks his femur playing in his second game in U17.

2014: Auston becomes a member of the US National Under-18 Team (U18)

2014: Phoenix Coyotes become Arizona Coyotes

2015: Auston and his mom and sister move to Switzerland so he can play for the Zurich Lions in Switzerland's National League

2016: Auston Matthews is selected first in the NHL Draft, by the Toronto Maple Leafs

2016: Auston sets a new record by scoring four goals in his first NHL game, against the Ottawa Senators

2016: Auston plays his first game against the Arizona Coyotes

2017: Auston scores his 40th goal in his first NHL season

2017: Auston wins, by a landslide, the Calder Memorial Trophy for NHL Rookie of the Year at the 2017 NHL awards

2017: Auston suffers a back injury and sits out several games

2018: Auston suffers a shoulder injury and, again, must sit out several games

Glossary

cystic fibrosis (CF) A serious genetic disease that mainly affects the digestive system and lungs

drafted A system of assigning new players to teams whereby exclusive rights to players are apportioned among professional teams

femur A long bone in the leg that extends from the hip to the knee; also called the thighbone

franchise A team and its operating organization which has the right to membership in a professional sports league

modern era In the NHL, the period starting from the 1930s onward, when the rules for professional hockey as it is played today were set

Pee-wee An age-specific level of youth sports

rookie A first-year participant in a major professional sport

sponsorship An agreement in which a person receives financial or other assistance from a sponsor, such as a company or organization, sometimes in exchange for promoting the sponsor publicly

tournaments Sports events in which a number of teams or players compete against one another until one is declared an overall winner

unanimous Having the agreement and consent of all

well-being The feeling of being happy, healthy, or prosperous

wing One of the offensive positions or players on either side of a center position in certain team sports

Find Out More

Books

Joyce, Gare. *Young Leafs: The Making of a New Hockey History.* Simon & Schuster, 2017.

Podnieks, Andrew. *Fast Ice: Superstars of the New NHL.* ECW Press, 2017.

Toronto Star. *100 Years in Blue and White: A Century of Hockey in Toronto.* Triumph Books, 2016.

Websites

For articles on Auston Matthews games:
www.NHL.com

The Internet Hockey Database:
www.hockeydb.com

The Toronto Maple Leafs official site:
www.nhl.com/mapleleafs

Auston Matthews on Twitter
https://twitter.com/am34?lang=en

Index

About the Author

Julia Sillett is an avid reader and writer. She has a master's degree in English and works in the public relations field. Her most creative ideas come to her when she's watching the sun rise or when she's walking to the park with her husband.